Toriyama Sensei gave me some pointers
on how to bow correctly.

I'm talking about how to draw someone bowing!!
(LOL)

—**Toyotarou, 2019**

Toyotarou

Toyotarou created the manga adaptation for the *Dragon Ball Z*
anime's 2015 film, *Dragon Ball Z: Resurrection F*. He is also the
author of the spin-off series *Dragon Ball Heroes: Victory Mission*,
which debuted in *V-Jump* in Japan in November 2012.

Akira Toriyama

Renowned worldwide for his playful, innovative storytelling and
humorous, distinctive art style, Akira Toriyama burst onto the manga
scene in 1980 with the wildly popular *Dr. Slump*. His hit series *Dragon Ball*
(published in the U.S. as *Dragon Ball* and *Dragon Ball Z*) ran from 1984
to 1995 in Shueisha's *Weekly Shonen Jump* magazine. He is also known
for his design work on video games such as *Dragon Quest*, *Chrono Trigger*,
Tobal No. 1 and *Blue Dragon*. His recent manga works include *COWA!*, *Kajika*,
Sand Land, *Neko Majin*, *Jaco the Galactic Patrolman* and a children's book,
Toccio the Angel. He lives with his family in Japan.

SHONEN JUMP Manga Edition

STORY BY **Akira Toriyama**
ART BY **Toyotarou**

TRANSLATION **Caleb Cook**
LETTERING **Brandon Bovia**
DESIGN **Joy Zhang**
EDITOR **Rae First**

DRAGON BALL SUPER © 2015 BY BIRD STUDIO, Toyotarou
All rights reserved. First published in Japan in 2015 by SHUEISHA Inc., Tokyo.
English translation rights arranged by SHUEISHA Inc.

The stories, characters and incidents mentioned
in this publication are entirely fictional.

Printed in Italy

Published by VIZ Media, LLC
P.O. Box 77010
San Francisco, CA 94107

10 9 8 7 6 5
First printing, December 2020
Fifth printing, November 2023

viz.com

PARENTAL ADVISORY
DRAGON BALL SUPER is rated T for
Teen and is recommended for ages 13
and up. This volume contains realistic
and fantasy violence.

DRAGON BALL SUPER

SUPER

GREAT ESCAPE

11

STORY BY
Akira Toriyama

ART BY
Toyotarou

CAST OF
CHARACTERS

God of Destruction Beerus

Guide Angel Whis

Piccolo

Majin Boo

Son Goku

Vegeta

Jaco

Bulma

Moro

Galactic Patrol Agent: Irico

Great Lord of Lords

Escaped Convict: Pasta

Esca

Galactic Patrol Agent: Merus

STORY THUS FAR

A long, long time ago, Son Goku left on a journey in search of the legendary Dragon Balls—a set of seven balls that, when gathered, would summon the dragon Shenlong to grant any wish. After a great adventure, he collects them all. Later, he becomes the apprentice of Kame-Sen'nin, fights a number of vicious enemies, defeats the great Majin Boo and restores peace on Earth. Some time passes, and then Lord Beerus, the God of Destruction, suddenly awakens and sets out in search of the Super Saiyan God. Goku, by becoming the Super Saiyan God, manages to stop Beerus from destroying the Earth and starts training under him with Vegeta. Then, our heroes travel to the future to fight Goku Black and Zamas of the parallel world. Soon after, the Lords of Everything decide to host a Tournament of Power featuring the strongest warriors from twelve universes. After some time, the ancient villain Moro escapes from the Galactic Prison and travels to New Namek in search of the Dragon Balls. Goku and Vegeta confront him, but are unable to prevent him from making his wishes. Moro's ability to absorb life energy seems like too much to handle, but now, Goku, Vegeta and the Great Lord of Lords slumbering inside Boo are off to confront Moro again!!

TABLE OF CONTENTS

CHAPTER 49: OUTER SPACE BATTLE

8

NOT SO FAST !!

FWSH

TCH!

FWP

WHFF

SHP

WHFF

FWAH!

FSU

12

SOME-
THING
SEEMS
OFF!

HIS
REAL
BODY
ISN'T
HERE...

W-
WHAT'S
GOING
ON?!

WMP
WMP
WMP
WMP
WMP

WHERE
IS HE
ABSORB-
ING THE
PLANET'S
ENERGY
FROM?!

CRAP!
WHERE'D
HE GO?!

GRp

O-OVER
THERE!!

WAIT,
KAKARROT
!!

UGH!

SAIYANS
CAN'T
SURVIVE
IN THE
VACUUM OF
SPACE!!

THAT'S
OUTER
SPACE!

I'LL
GO.

OH
RIGHT
...

!

DAMMIT... THERE'S NO WAY TO TELL HOW THE BATTLE IS GOING!!

DARN IT. THEY'RE OUT OF SIGHT!!

FSHH

AGENT MERUS! MORO AND THE GREAT LORD OF LORDS HAVE LEFT NAMEK'S ORBIT.

PERHAPS THE FIGHT HAS BEGUN?!

NAMEK'S NOT LOSING ENERGY ANYMORE.

FIRST, WE ATTEND TO GOKU AND VEGETA!

GOKU AND VEGETA REMAIN IN THE ATMOSPHERE. WHICH PARTY SHOULD WE GO AFTER THEM?

HEF!

HEF!

...BUT NOW THAT MY POWER EXCEEDS YOURS, THEY NO LONGER TROUBLE ME.

I WAS CONFUSED BY YOUR STRANGE POWERS...

HMPH!

!

BECAUSE THIS IS UN-IMPRESSIVE.

DID SOMETHING HAPPEN TO YOU THESE PAST TEN MILLION YEARS?

RESIST AND I'LL SEAL OFF YOUR MAGIC AGAIN!

LISTEN, MORO-- YOU'RE GOING TO COME QUIETLY BACK TO GALACTIC PRISON.

!

GRP

GO AHEAD. DO YOUR WORST.

THE OLD SEALING TECHNIQUE, IS IT?

HEH HEH ...

...

...

...

NO, I THOUGHT NOT. I DON'T SENSE THE SAME GOD POWER YOU ONCE HELD.

YOU'RE SHARP.

...

I DARESAY YOU LACK THE POWER TO UNLEASH THE SEALING SPELL, RIGHT?

24

AT THIS RATE, HE'LL BE TOO MUCH FOR US TO HANDLE SOON!

AND WHAT ABOUT THAT MAGIC SEALING TECHNIQUE?

HOW INFURI-ATING.

H-HEY... DID YOU JUST FEEL MORO GETTING EVEN STRONGER ?!

BWOOM

COME ABOARD.

GOKU, VEGETA.

ZOOSH

WHAT DO YOU MEAN?!

IN FACT, I SUSPECT THAT AS HE IS NOW, THE GREAT LORD OF LORDS CAN'T EXECUTE THE KAI KAI-MATORU.

NO...

I GUESS HE CAN'T SHOOT OFF THE SEALING MOVE UNLESS MORO'S BEING HELD IN PLACE?

W-WAIT, WASN'T THAT OUR ACE IN THE HOLE?!

IT OCCURRED TO ME EARLIER WHEN BOO ATTEMPTED TO USE IT.

...BECAUSE OF THE **SPLITTING** THAT BOO UNDERWENT.

IT'S MOST LIKELY...

INDEED IT WAS...

EXPLAIN YOURSELF.

THAT PINK GUY'S KINDA CREEPY. ONE TIME I EVEN SAW HIM SPROUT EXTRA ARMS FROM HIS BODY...

YES...

YOU MEAN THE SPLIT BETWEEN HIS GOOD AND EVIL HALVES?

WHAT **CAN'T** THAT WEIRDO DO?

HE SPLIT?!

SO THE GOD POWER WAS PASSED ON TO THE EVIL HALF OF BOO?

I SUSPECT SO.

MORE FUSING, HUH? LOTTA THAT GOING AROUND...

HUH? SERIOUSLY?

AND WHILE WE CAN'T SPLIT, WE CAN ASSIMILATE.

WELL, MY PEOPLE CAN REGROW LOST LIMBS.

THAT LITTLE GUY HAD ACTUAL GOD POWER IN HIM?

TCH...

BECAUSE THE GOOD BOO INHERITED THE GREAT LORD OF LORDS'S PHYSICAL APPEARANCE, I ASSUMED HE RECEIVED THE GOD POWER AS WELL, BUT MAYBE THAT POWER WENT TO THE EVIL BOO INSTEAD.

GAH...

DID SOME-ONE STEAL YOUR POWER ...

...AND REDUCE YOU TO THAT PINK, PIGGISH FORM FROM EARLIER?

KRSHH

KRSHH

KRAK

FLIP

DAM-MIT!

WHA

WHEN HE WAS OBLITERATED, SO WAS MY POWER...

I SEE.

...!

HOW WONDER-FUL IT IS NOT TO HAVE TO FEAR THAT ANYMORE.

...IT'S CLEAR TO ME THAT NO BEING IN THIS UNIVERSE POSSESSES THE POWER TO SEAL AWAY MY MAGIC.

NOW THAT I'VE TAKEN A GLIMPSE AT THOSE LATENT MEMO-RIES...

IT WAS ALWAYS GOING TO TAKE BRUTE FORCE TO BRING DOWN THIS FOE.

GIMMICKY TECHNIQUES LIKE THAT NEVER ACTUALLY GET THE JOB DONE.

I THINK VEGETA'S RIGHT...

MORO! DEAD AHEAD!

...WHICH IS WHY WE GOTTA DO SOMETHING NOW.

DAMMIT... WE'RE COMPLETELY POWERLESS IN OUTER SPACE!

BOOM

RRMMM

YEP.

NATURALLY. MAGIC ASIDE, WE ARE THE STRONGER FIGHTERS. JUST ONE OF US AT FULL POWER IN SUPER SAIYAN BLUE FORM COULD HANDLE HIM.

ARE YOU ABSOLUTELY CERTAIN THAT THE TWO OF YOU ARE MORE POWERFUL THAN MORO?

GOKU! VEGETA!

BWOOMP

IN THAT CASE, I WILL DRAG MORO BACK TO THE SURFACE OF PLANET NAMEK, WHERE YOU TWO CAN FINISH THE JOB.

ROGER THAT.

KLK

?

I'M OFF.

IS THAT ONE OF THEM SPACE SUITS? !

PLEASE RETURN TO NAMEK IN THE MEAN-TIME.

BWOOOM

HFF HFF HFF

CAN ALL YOUR OUTFITS DO THAT?

NAH, THAT ONE WAS CUSTOM-MADE FOR MERUS.

CAN'T. WON'T. I'M WAY SCARED OF OUTER SPACE, MAN.

SO YOU'RE NOT BACKING HIM UP, JACO?

36

ZOOM

GRAP

ZOOM

TMP

I CAN'T WIN ALONE.

YES, OF COURSE.

WE NEED TO GET MORO BACK TO NAMEK SOMEHOW SO THAT THE TEAM CAN BATTLE HIM TOGETHER!

TH-THANK YOU.

ARE YOU STILL WITH US, GREAT LORD OF LORDS?

EXCELLENT. WHEN THE TIME COMES...

AS A LORD OF LORDS, YES, I CAN.

YOU KNOW YOUR STUFF.

BEFORE THAT, CAN I CONFIRM SOMETHING WITH YOU?

CAN YOU STILL USE INSTANT TELEPORTATION?

BLASTED GALACTIC PATROL!!

YOU AGAIN!!

...THAT'S ENOUGH!!

SHOON

I SAID...

ZOOSH

BOOM

FWP

M-MY EYES!!

C-CURSE YOU!

TMP

!

GRp

I'VE GOT YOU NOW!

FWp

LET'S GO AFTER HIM, VEGETA!!

I'M SENSING MORO'S CHI BACK ON NAMEK NOW!

AH!

!

SPOT ON!

FWP

THANKS A LOT, MERUS!

48

FSH

WE'RE AT FULL POWER NOW, SO YOU WON'T GET AWAY AGAIN.

MORO! READY FOR A FAIR FIGHT?

...

WE MUST HURRY BACK TO NAMEK TOO.

PFFT, DON'T WORRY.

YOU WERE AWESOME OUT THERE, MERUS!

WOOM!

BEEP

YES, I GUESS SO.

CUZ, Y'KNOW, THEY'RE A TEENY TINY BIT STRONGER THAN ME.

THOSE TWO WILL HAVE THAT GUY BEAT BEFORE WE KNOW IT.

IT STILL HOLDS ENERGY? WHAT A WASTE TO LEAVE FOOD ON MY PLATE.

AH, PLANET NAMEK...

HEH HEH...

...

WE'RE ABOUT TO DESTROY YOU ONCE AND FOR ALL!

I DON'T THINK YOU COMPREHEND THE SITUATION.

THE THIRD WISH!

?

SO FOOLISH. SO NAIVE.

HA HA HA!

YOU SEEM TO HAVE FORGOTTEN SOMETHING QUITE IMPORTANT.

!

51

CHAPTER 50: GREAT ESCAPE

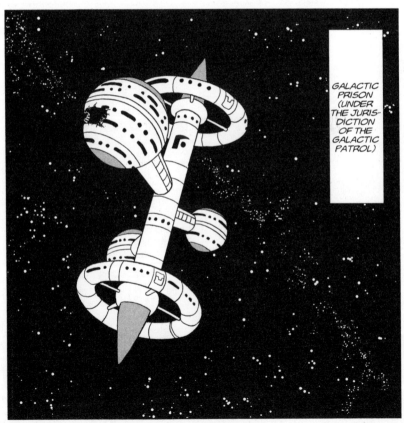

GALACTIC
PRISON
(UNDER
THE JURIS-
DICTION
OF THE
GALACTIC
PATROL)

HE MELTED THE BARS...

THAT MORO GUY'S MAGIC IS SCARY. IT EVEN GOT HIM OUT OF **THIS** PRISON!

KLNK

YEAH, SINCE CAPTAIN MERUS SET OUT TO RECAPTURE MORO, WE GOTTA HAVE THINGS IN TIP-TOP SHAPE ON OUR END.

AND THE GALACTIC KING WANTS THIS REPAIRED QUICKLY? THAT'S A TALL ORDER...

NAH, MORO'S THE ONE TO WATCH OUT FOR. THE OTHERS COULD NEVER ESCAPE ON THEIR OWN.

MAYBE WE SHOULD BE WARY OF THE **OTHER** PRISONERS HERE INSTEAD.

NO CLUE. BUT FOR NOW, WE JUST GOTTA BELIEVE IN THE GALACTIC PATROL.

BUT MORO WAS ALREADY ABLE TO BREAK THROUGH THE PRISON'S SUPERSTRONG DEFENSES. WHAT'LL STOP HIM FROM DOING THAT AGAIN?

TMP TMP

GET IN!

VWOOM

56

HOW MANY TIMES DO WE GOTTA LOCK YOU THREE UP? CAN'T YOU LEARN YOUR LESSON FOR ONCE?

THEY MUST ACTUALLY LOVE IT IN HERE.

FREAKING UNBELIEVABLE.

KCHK

TCH...

A LIFE OF CRIME'S THE ONLY KIND FOR US.

HMPH!

VWOOM

GLOW

ZOOM

NEW NAMEK

ZOOOM

GLINT

KA ZAM

HUH? WHAT'S HAPPEN-ING?!

KZZT KZZT

KZZT KZZT

61

TOMP

TOMP
TOMP

WHAT THE HECK'S GOING ON?!

SHOOT, I CAN'T GET AHOLD OF GALACTIC PATROL HQ!

B-BACK IN YOUR CELLS, INMATES!!

WHAT DO YOU THINK YOU'RE DOING?!

AH... AHH.

Y-YIKES!!

I KNOW OUR SPACESHIP'S HERE, SO YOU'RE GONNA HAND IT OVER, 'KAY?

W-WHAT ABOUT US, BIG BRO?

!

...

LET'S JOIN THE PARTY.

THIS COULD GET FUN...

WE AIN'T GONNA HURT YA.

THE REST OF YOU ARE COMING ALONG TOO!

BEEP BEEP BEEP

IN-INCOMING!

O-OH NO...

WHAT'S THE SITUATION?!

THERE'S AN EMERGENCY DISPATCH STRAIGHT FROM HQ!

WHAT?! WHAT HAPPENED?

SAY WHAT?!

...HAVE STAGED A MASSIVE PRISON BREAK!

THE INMATES AT THE GALACTIC PRISON...

I'M REMEM-BERING...

AH... AHH...

ONE MENT AGO? THAT WAS RIGHT ABOUT WHEN MORO MADE HIS WISH, RIGHT?!

YES, THE MESSAGE CAME LATE BECAUSE WE LOST CONTACT WITH THE PRISON...

AND THE INCIDENT ACTUALLY OCCURRED ONE MENT AGO.

IN THAT CASE...

O-OH YEAH. THEY BRAIN-WASHED YOU AND FORCED YOU TO STATE THEIR WISHES, RIGHT?

YES...

HMM? REMEM-BERING WHAT?

THE FINAL ONE!

MORO'S WISH...

...THAT EVERY PRISONER IN THE GALACTIC PRISON GO FREE.

YES, FOR THAT FINAL WISH, I DEMANDED...

ZZRRRM

I'M FEELING A LOT OF CHI SIGNATURES IN THERE!!

A SPACESHIP?! IS IT THEM...?!

BWOOM

LOOK OUT!!

HUH?

BWOOM

THE ONES INSIDE... I JUST FELT THEIR CHI GROW!

I THINK MORO MUST'VE USED HIS MAGIC AGAIN!

SHP

SHP

SHP

WHRRR

TOMP

TOMP

ARRRGH!!

WE HAD NO IDEA HE'D BE BRINGING FRIENDS...

SO THIS IS WHY HE SEEMED SO CONFIDENT.

...MY CON-VICTS.

HAVE AT THEM...

BO

F

T

O

M

GAHH!!

Bw Bw Bw Bw

FLIK

RMMBL

HOW'RE THEY THIS STRONG?!

W-WHOA, THESE AIN'T YOUR EVERYDAY GALACTIC PATROL GUYS!

...

SO GO! THEY CAN'T HOLD YOU ALL OFF AT ONCE.

UNLESS YOU WANNA HEAD BACK TO THE SLAMMER, YOU'D BETTER OBEY LORD MORO'S COMMANDS!

KEEP GOING AT 'EM!

HEY! DON'T TURN YELLOW ON ME!

POW POW POW

ZOOOM

BWOOM

HUH?

GOD FORM?!

HUH?

BWOOM

MORO'S STARTED ABSORBING ENERGY AGAIN!!

SKFF

POW

THE MOMENT WE DROP OUR GUARD, OUR TRANSFORM- ATIONS FAIL US!

TCH!

SHOOM

SHOOM

YOU OKAY, BOO?!

UGHH ...

SKF SKF

SLAM

WHAM

DARN ...

THAT BATTLE AGAINST MORO IN SPACE EARLIER MUST HAVE TAKEN A TOLL ON HIM.

POW POW POW

KA WHAM WHAM

WHAM WHAM

TO CREATE AN IDEAL GALAXY WHERE I AM FREE TO CONSUME PLANETS AS I WISH.

WHAT'RE YOU REALLY AFTER HERE?

WHAT'S THE POINT OF ALL THIS?

MO-RO !!

H-HEY !!

GATHERING THESE ALLIES IS ONE SMALL STEP TOWARD THAT END.

...I DETEST THE SORT OF PEACE THAT YOU PEOPLE SEEK TO PRESERVE ON THIS PLANET AND OTHERS.

WHAT I CAN SAY IS...

DO YOU HOLD A GRUDGE AGAINST THE GALACTIC PATROL THEN?

I WON-DER.

...

...SHOULD BE ERADI-CATED.

ALL WHO WOULD STRIVE FOR SUCH NON-SENSE...

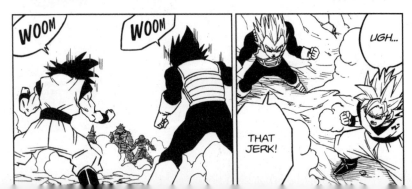

WOOM

WOOM

UGH...

THAT JERK!

DAMMIT! HOW MANY TIMES WILL WE FALL FOR HIS TRICKS?!

AND NOW WE CAN'T EVEN GO SUPER SAIYAN...

ZOOOM

WHAM WHAM

BY "WE," YOU MEAN ME TOO?

HUH?

WE HAVE TO HELP OUR ALLIES, AGENT JACO!

THE CONVICTS HAVE ALL GATHERED HERE!

OH NO!

I CAN HELP AS WELL!

I...

84

I CAN'T FIGHT, BUT AT LEAST I CAN HEAL YOUR INJURIES!

ZAP ZAP ZAP

ZAP

MORO MUST ONLY BE ABSORBING ENERGY FROM US!

BLAST! THESE FOOLS AREN'T GETTING ANY WEAKER...

THUD THUD

TMP TMP

86

FWP

WE'LL MEET AT YOUR HQ.

VERY WELL.

...

GRAB ON TO ME, AGENT MERUS!

YOU TOO, VEGETA!

IF HE ABSORBS ANY MORE ENERGY, I WON'T BE ABLE TO USE INSTANT TELEPORTA-TION AGAIN!

WHAT'S THE HOLD-UP?

STUPID GOD POWER...

STUPID MAGIC SPELLS...

...?

PEW
PEW
PEW

PEW PEW PEW

AND YET, I'VE BEEN REDUCED TO THIS!!

WE SAIYANS PRIDE OUR-SELVES ON OUR PHYSICAL MIGHT. A WARRIOR RACE HAS NO NEED FOR FANCY PARLOR TRICKS!!

FORGET INSTANT TELEPOR-TATION!!

LET'S GO! YOU WANNA DIE HERE OR SOMETHING?!

HEY!

WHAP

ACK!

ZOOM

GO AHEAD, KAKAR-ROT.

WHOOPSIE !!

KLAK

THIS IS WHERE WE PART WAYS.

VEGETA!!

ZOOM

OH
NO!

KACHK

KACHK

IT'S
NOW OR
NEVER,
GOKU!!

SKF

SKF

BWAM

FWP

DAM-
MIT!!

SLAM SLAM SLAM SLAM

WHERE'D
THEY RUN
OFF TO?!

!

THEY'RE
GONE?

HUH?

OPEN UP.

ZOOM

GALACTIC PATROL HQ

BWUH?!

FSH

APOLOGIES FOR INTERRUPTING YOUR ROYAL BATH, GALACTIC KING!!

...

SORRY, MISTER. YOURS WAS THE ONLY CHI I COULD SENSE.

W-WHAT THE HECK?!

I DUNNO... WHAT COULD HE BE THINKING?

WHAT DO YOU THINK VEGETA MEANT BY ALL THAT?

DODGING ALL OUR SHOTS.

DAMMIT!

TCH!

PEW

PEW

YOU MIGHT WANT TO GRAB HOLD OF SOMETHING.

THIS WILL GET BUMPY.

BEEP BEEP

VWOOO

KACHK

ZOOOON

WHAT'RE YOU IDIOTS DOING?!

W-WE LOST 'EM.

96

WE'RE HEADING BACK TO GALACTIC PATROL HQ TOO.

BEEP

PHEW...

BY THE SKIN OF OUR TEETH.

NOOM

WE'RE GOING TO PLANET YARDRAT.

FWIP

HUH?

W-WHERE'S THAT EXACTLY?

NO. YOU'RE GOING TO FLY THIS THING WHERE I WANT TO GO.

CHAPTER 51: TO EACH THEIR OWN PLANS

PHEW...

THE WHOLE PLANET DIED BEFORE WE KNEW IT!

W-WOW...

ZOOSH

GALACTIC
PATROL
HQ

PLEASE, PUT SOMETHING ON!!

G-GALACTIC KING, WHAT AN UNBECOMING LOOK FOR YOU!!

IS IT TRUE THAT EVERY LAST INMATE FROM THE GALACTIC PRISON HAS ESCAPED?!

H-HEY!!

SLAM

WHY WASN'T I TOLD?

H-HERE, YOUR ROYAL CROWN!

EEK!

I THOUGHT YOU KNEW, YOUR HIGH-NESS...

PLOP

ARE YOU BLIND? HIS ROYALNESS HAS GOT HIS KINGLY CROWN ON!

ISN'T HE STILL NAKED?

WE HAD SOME OF OUR IN-TEL WIRES CROSSED HERE AT HQ.

I, UHHH...

HUH?

LET ME GUESS, YOU THINK I'VE BEEN WEARING PANTS THIS WHOLE TIME?

GOKU!

PSST. HEY.

DID BOO AND A LITTLE GREEN KID SHOW UP HERE EARLIER?

A CHILD?

ACTU-ALLY...

YOU'RE ALL RIGHT!

HEYA, ESCA!

I'M SO GLAD YOU WERE ABLE TO TELEPORT AWAY!

HMM? WHERE'S BOO?

YES!

UM, I DON'T SEE VEGETA WITH YOU.

BOO FOUGHT HARD OUT THERE FOR US. HE MUST BE WORN-OUT.

AFTER WE ARRIVED, HIS FACE CHANGED BACK AND HE FELL ASLEEP.

ZZZ ZZZ

I BET HE FLEW OFF TO TRAIN SOMEWHERE.

DON'T WORRY-- HE'S PROBABLY FINE.

WE CAN'T SIT ON OUR HANDS EITHER. ANYONE GOT A PLAN?

ONE THAT DOESN'T INVOLVE BOO?

ZZZ ZZZ

OUR NORMAL TACTICS DIDN'T WORK AGAINST MORO AT ALL, AND I'M THINKING THAT HIT VEGETA PRETTY HARD. HE MUST HAVE A NEW IDEA IN THE WORKS.

TO TRAIN, YOU SAY?

MORO DOESN'T SEEM TO BE PURSUING US. HE'S FLOWN OFF IN ANOTHER DIRECTION.

I CAN'T SENSE HIS CHI ANYMORE EITHER.

IT'S AS IF HE FLEW AWAY AT TOP SPEED.

THE GUY WHO WAS AT MORO'S SIDE.

SAGAN-BO?

...SO I CAN'T TRACK IT BY RADAR.

SAGANBO'S SHIP IS THE FASTEST I'VE EVER KNOWN...

HE'S THE LEADER OF A GANG OF BANDITS THAT ONCE RAMPAGED AROUND THE GALAXY.

AUTOPILOT ACTIVATED.

HIS STRENGTH MADE HIM TOUGH TO CAPTURE.

AH, THE ONE WHO DEALT A BLOW TO KAKARROT?

YOU'RE A FATHER?

OH?

WITHOUT MORO AIDING HIM, EVEN MY BOY COULD DEFEAT HIM.

THAT FOOL WAS NO WORTHY OPPONENT.

AND NOW HE'S FREE AGAIN.

SO WHAT IF I AM?

JUST UNEXPECTED. THAT'S ALL...

ERM...

SPEAKING IN TERMS OF YOUR EARTH TIME... ABOUT ONE WEEK.

NEVER MIND THAT. HOW MUCH FARTHER TO YARDRAT?

LET ME PLUG IN THE NUMBERS...

UM, VEGETA.

I'LL BE RESTING IN THE MEANTIME.

ALL RIGHT.

110

A FEW DAYS PASS IN THE GALAXY...

I WILL ACHIEVE VICTORY NEXT TIME.

OVER MORO, OVER THOSE CONVICTS...

I CAN'T AFFORD TO BE MADE A FOOL OF LIKE THAT AGAIN.

...AND OVER KAKARROT.

PLANET
ZOON

RMMMBL

W- WHATEVER HAPPENS, WE GOTTA PROTECT THE ROYAL TREASURE.

ZOON

SHWP

TMP TMP

LET'S GO.

FWAH

WE'VE GOT ALL THE TREASURE FROM THIS PLANET.

SORRY ABOUT THE WAIT, LORD MORO.

SHOOM SHOOM

AND NOW IT'S MEAL-TIME.

WELL DONE.

GULP

NO MATTER HOW MANY PLANETS I WATCH DIE, IT STILL SENDS A CHILL DOWN MY SPINE.

WE SNAG THE LOOT, AND YOU GET TO CHOW DOWN ON THE PLANET-- WE MAKE A PERFECT TEAM, HUH?

THANK YOU.

NOT A BAD PLANET.

HMM...

AND YOU WILL SURELY NEED RESOURCES OF VALUE ONCE MY IDEALS ARE REALIZED.

INDEED.

INCOMING CALL FROM SOME OF OUR SCOUTS.

WHAT IS IT?

BZZT

SNAGGING VALUABLES IS OUR SPECIALTY, SO DON'T YOU WORRY.

WE FOUND A PLANET WITH SOME NICE ENERGY, I THINK.

SAGANBO!

WH AK

BWO OM

SO IT'S OUR JOB TO STRIP THIS PLANET OF ITS TREASURES BEFORE THEY SHOW UP!

GWARR!

IT'S CRAWLING WITH ENERGETIC BEASTIES.

GREAT. WE'LL HEAD YOUR WAY.

AND WE'LL BE WAITING.

SHWP

THE WHOLE SQUAD'S COMING TO US, LADIES.

HEY.

BEEP

THUD

THE PROBLEM IS THEY'RE MOVING AT SUCH HIGH SPEEDS THAT WE KEEP LOSING THEM ON THE RADAR.

DID YOU MANAGE TO LOCK ONTO THEIR LIFE SIGNATURES?

THEY'VE PROGRESSED THAT FAR ALREADY?!

...PLANET ZOON HAS BEEN ANNIHILATED.

IT SEEMS...

...MORO HIMSELF HAS GOTTEN EVEN STRONGER.

AND AFTER A FEW DAYS OF THIS...

AND I CAN'T READ CHI SIGNATURES THAT FAR AWAY.

SO THAT WON'T WORK.

I SUSPECT THAT MORO IS GOING AFTER PLANETS BEYOND OUR IMMEDIATE REACH...

DAMMIT... EVEN IF WE COULD CONFRONT MORO NOW... OUR ODDS OF VICTORY ARE VIRTUALLY ZERO.

EVEN IF **YOU** WERE FIGHTING SERIOUSLY?

HUH?

W- WHOA THERE, GOKU!

THAT'S WHY I DODGED.

YES?

I THREW THAT PUNCH MEANING TO CONNECT.

DID AGENT MERUS SAY SOMETHING THAT MADE YA MAD?

I KNOW AGENT MERUS CAN BE A SNOBBISH, PRETENTIOUS, HEAVY-HANDED LEADER--I GET IT. BUT HE AIN'T ALL BAD.

WE'RE ALL FRIENDS HERE.

COME ON, GUYS.

I WANNA GET A FEEL FOR YOUR TRUE POWER, MERUS.

THE WAY THOSE BANGS ARE CHOPPED JUST A LITTLE TOO SHORT?

AND LOOK AT HIS FACE. IT'S KINDA ADORABLE, YEAH?

HMM?

I KNOW JUST THE PLACE.

VERY WELL.

SPAR WITH ME?

YOU GUYS EVEN GOT ONE OF THESE, HUH?

OOH...

...BUILT TO WITH- STAND A DECENT AMOUNT OF ABUSE.

THIS IS A TRAINING ROOM JUST FOR US AGENTS ...

FWAH

YOU PEOPLE SPEND TIME ON THAT?

FITNESS?

INSTEAD OF WASTING TIME WITH THIS.

IS THAT ALL? WE SHOULD JUST SHOW HIM THIS YEAR'S PHYSICAL FITNESS RESULTS.

GOKU IS JUST TESTING MERUS'S POWER.

WHERE'S THE BLOODLUST?

WOW...

IF YOU'RE CURIOUS, I HOLD THE TITLE FOR BEST UPWARD-FACING DOG POSE, THREE YEARS RUNNING.

HOW ABOUT YOU TRAIN ME?

I'VE GOT IT!

?

AND IT'S JUST LIKE I THOUGHT.

!

TRAIN-ING?

HMM? WHAT'D THAT CRAZY GOKU JUST SAY?

...IT SEEMS LIKE YOU KNOW PLENTY THAT I DON'T.

I STILL DON'T HAVE A TOTAL FEEL FOR YOUR STRENGTH, BUT...

AM I WRONG?

IT'S ALL ABOUT LETTING THE BODY MOVE ON INSTINCT, SO IT MIGHT WORK AGAINST MORO EVEN WHEN HE STARTS ABSORBING MY ENERGY.

THERE'S A MOVE THAT I'M STILL TRYING TO MASTER.

I'VE GOT A FEELING THAT TRAINING WITH YOU COULD GET ME CLOSER TO MASTERING IT.

GREAT!

I AM ALL TOO HAPPY TO ASSIST.

...

THEN THAT IS WHAT WE SHALL DO.

PHEW! CUZ IT IT'S NOT REAL TRAINING IF I CAN'T EVEN SWITCH TO GOD MODE.

BUT THIS ROOM CAN ONLY TAKE SO MUCH, SO I RECOMMEND ANOTHER LOCATION FOR YOUR TRAINING.

PLANET JUNG

HAND OVER ALL THE BLUE AURUM YOU FOLKS'VE PROCESSED.

THAT SAFE AIN'T GONNA OPEN ITSELF.

NOBODY'S SWOOPING IN TO SAVE THE DAY THIS TIME.

HA HA HA! TOO BAD FOR YOU, THE GALACTIC PATROL'S KINDA CLOSED FOR REPAIRS AT THE MOMENT.

W-WEREN'T YOU SCOUNDRELS ARRESTED BY THE GALACTIC PATROL?

LATER!

BANG BANG

GAH!

YOU GOT IT!

CALL SAGAN-BO, GHETTI. GIVE HIM A GOOD STORY.

LUCKY BREAK FOR US, HUH? THE WHOLE GALAXY'S OURS FOR THE TAKING, AND ALL IT TOOK WAS PRETENDING TO PLEDGE LOYALTY TO THAT MORO FELLA.

WHICH PLANET SHOULD WE PAY A VISIT TO NEXT?

BEEP

THIS PLANET WAS A BUST. NOT MUCH ENERGY, NO SIR. WE'RE OFF TO SEARCH FOR AN-OTHER.

CAPTAIN SAGAN-BO? THAT YOU?

ZOOSH

WHAT'S THAT?

BRO, REMEMBER WHEN MERUS AND HIS MERRY GANG SHOWED UP TO HAUL US IN? I'M REMEMBERING SOMETHING THEY SAID.

THAT'S WHAT IT SOUNDED LIKE.

WELL, WELL... SO THIS EARTH PLACE HAS GOT ITS OWN STASH OF BLUE AURUM?

THAT PUNY AGENT OF THEIRS SAID THAT ON SOME PLANET CALLED EARTH, THEY CALL BLUE AURUM SKY-GOLD INSTEAD.

LET'S AMBLE ON OVER TO EARTH.

WELL WHAT'RE WE WAITING FOR?

YOU HEARD THEM FROM WAY UP THERE? KILLER PAIR OF EARS ON YOU, SIS.

WAKE UP, VEGETA! WE'VE ARRIVED!

AT THAT MOMENT, VEGETA FINALLY MADE IT TO YARDRAT...

CHAPTER 52: GOKU AND VEGETA'S TRAINING

I HEAR THEY COME IN MULTIPLE TYPES.

SO THESE ARE THE YARDRAT-IANS. I'VE NEVER EN-COUNTERED THEM BEFORE.

MOVE ASIDE, FOLKS.

TMP

TMP

TMP

TMP

TMP

146

WELCOME!

HOWDY!

YOU LOOK QUITE SIMPLE FOR A SAIYAN.

GRP

!

WE HEARD ALL ABOUT YOU FROM GOKU!

YOU MUST BE VEGETA!

OH...

UH, THIS IS VEGETA.

147

SO WE'RE ETERNALLY GRATEFUL TO YOU AND GOKU FOR TAKING CARE OF THAT PROBLEM.

YOU'RE WELCOME.

I REMEMBER HEARING THEY'D ATTACKED THIS PLACE.

THE GINYU SQUAD CAUSED QUITE A STIR ON OUR PLANET BEFORE GOKU DEFEATED THEM.

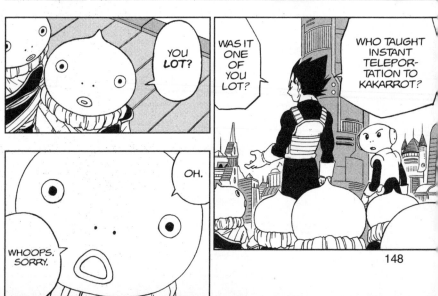

YOU LOT?

WAS IT ONE OF YOU LOT?

WHO TAUGHT INSTANT TELEPORTATION TO KAKARROT?

OH.

WHOOPS. SORRY.

148

HUH?

I'M HERE ON MY OWN.

...WAS ME.

THE ONE WHO TAUGHT GOKU INSTANT TELEPORTATION...

...

WE'RE RATHER WEAK.

WHERE'D THEY ALL GO?

COME ON IN AND MEET THE ELDER.

COPIES?

SO SOMETIMES WE MAKE COPIES OF OURSELVES TO TRICK PEOPLE.

WHR R R R

AH, I'M NOT VEGETA. HE IS.

YOU LOOK QUITE SIMPLE FOR A SAIYAN.

GRP

ALLOW ME TO INTRODUCE ELDER PYBARA.

YOU MUST BE VEGETA.

YES, SO DO YOU HAVE A TECHNIQUE TO MAKE THAT HAPPEN?

WELL, I THINK I UNDERSTAND. YOU'RE HOPING TO BEAT THIS MORO FELLOW.

WHAT?

WE ARE NOT BLESSED WITH SOME GREAT WEALTH OF TECHNIQUES.

THERE'S BEEN A MISUNDERSTANDING, I'M AFRAID.

150

HUH...?

THAT'S YOUR NORMAL SIZE?

EVEN GIGANTIFICATION.

FWOOMP

VERY WELL.

STUDY HOW THE SPIRIT FUNCTIONS AND THE PATH WILL OPEN TO YOU AS WELL.

EVERYONE ON YARDRAT CAN DO THESE THINGS.

THESE ARE ACHIEVED BY SHIFTING, SPLITTING AND GROWING ONE'S VERY SPIRIT.

...THIS SO-CALLED SPIRIT CONTROL.

TEACH ME...

ROGER THAT! WE'LL HANDLE THINGS HERE.

I'LL BE AWAY FROM HQ FOR A BIT. CONTACT ME IF YOU NEED ANYTHING.

A FEW DAYS AFTER VEGETA LANDED ON YARDRAT, GOKU TRAVELED TO ANOTHER PLANET TO TRAIN WITH MERUS.

HMM...

WITH VEGETA MISSING AND GOKU TRAINING WITH MERUS, WE'RE CLEARLY SHORT HANDED.

WITH NO MAJOR CHANGES TO SPEAK OF, TIME PASSED UNPRODUCTIVELY AT HQ.

WE JUST DISPATCHED AGENTS TO PLANET RICCI. WE'RE RUNNING LOW ON PERSONNEL...

LOOKS LIKE THE CONVICTS SHOWED UP ON PLANET CHIP!

WE'RE IN NEED OF NEW RECRUITS, THEN...

YOU MEAN PEOPLE WHO'D COME WILLINGLY, RIGHT?

Y-YEAH ...

HOW ABOUT THE SECTOR YOU MANAGE, JACO?

OF COURSE! MONAKA!

AH!

WHAP

WHAT ABOUT THAT OTHER WARRIOR FROM THE MATCH AGAINST UNIVERSE 6? WHERE IS HE? COULD WE SUMMON HIM HERE?

NAMEKIAN, YOU SAY?

...

NO! I MEAN THE NAMEKIAN.

THE SANCTUARY

...

THAT COULD BE IT, UN-LESS...

OUR TELEPATHY DOES HAVE ITS LIMITS. THAT'S JUST HOW IT IS.

I CAN'T REACH ANYONE ON NEW NAMEK...

NO GOOD.

IF NOTHING ELSE, I'M CERTAIN THAT SOMETHING TERRIBLE IS HAPPENING OUT IN SPACE.

...

...THE NAMEKIANS CAPABLE OF TELEPATHY ARE ALL DEAD.

HUH... Y-YOU DON'T MEAN...?

LOOK THERE.

THAT'S EARTH.

PRETTY AS A PICTURE.

HERE'S HOPING IT'S GOT PLENTY OF BLUE AURUM.

YOU SAID IT.

FIRST, LET'S FIND A PLACE TO LAND.

SHARP
SHOOT-
ING.

BOOM BOOM BOOM

RMMMBL

WOOSH

WOOOSH

ABOVE US!!

UP THERE!

WHERE'D HE GO?

WHAT?

BRO! HE'S GONE!!

HRM?

...IS THIS GUY?

WH-WHO THE HECK...

TERRIBLE MANNERS FOR A GUEST.

SHOOTING FIRST WITHOUT ASKING QUESTIONS?

VWOOM

THEY CERTAINLY DON'T SEEM LIKE BIG THREATS.

BULMA!

DENDE, HOW'S IT GOING?

IS PICCOLO AROUND?

WHAT BRINGS YOU HERE?

CAPSULE

WE JUST GOT WORD FROM JACO.

CAN I HELP YOU?

HE JUST LEFT.

PICCO-LO?

HE'S COMING HERE TO DRAFT PICCOLO INTO THE GALACTIC PATROL.

...JACO DIRECT-LY?

...WHY DON'T WE ASK...

IS THE GALACTIC PATROL BATTLING SOMEONE OR SOMETHING AT THE MOMENT?

HUH?

PLEASE TELL ME EVERYTHING YOU KNOW.

I DON'T HAVE THE DETAILS, BUT...

165

KABOOM

DASH

168

TOO BAD FOR YOU, I'M MORE THAN USED TO THAT MOVE.

GAHHH!!

WH AP

WH AP

G- GET OFFA ME!!

FWIIP

YEOWCH...

URGH...

THUD

W-WHAT'S WITH THIS PLANET?

HOW'D IT COME TO BE HOME TO A POWERFUL BEING LIKE THIS?

O-OH NO.

HOW AWFUL.

AND THAT SAME TRAGEDY'S PLAYING OUT OVER AND OVER ACROSS THE GALAXY.

GET IT? NAMEK IS A DEAD PLANET NOW...

I'M HEADING YOUR WAY, SO GATHER THEM UP, OKAY?

MAYBE ALSO SON GOKU'S SON, OR THOSE BALDIES?

AND SINCE VEGETA AND GOKU ARE OFF TRAINING, YOU'RE COMING TO PICCOLO FOR HELP?

DARN RIGHT.

MY FELLOW NAMEKIANS...

YOU EARTHLINGS MAY BE TOTAL WIMPY WEAKLINGS, BUT ALL THOSE LIFE-FORMS YOU'VE GOT WOULD MAKE YOUR PLANET A TANTALIZING TREAT FOR MORO. HE'LL GOBBLE THE PLACE UP ONCE HE FINDS OUT.

PLANETS FOR MORO TO EAT.

AND BE ON ALERT! MORO SENT A BUNCH OF SCOUTS OUT INTO THE GALAXY.

KURIRIN AND TEN-SHINHAN? YOU GOT IT.

WHAT'RE THEY LOOKING FOR?

OH YEAH?

HMM? UM... THEY'D COME IN GROUPS OF TWO OR THREE IN A LONG, THIN SPACESHIP.

HOW WOULD WE RECOGNIZE THESE SCOUTS?

OH NO, WHAT IF...

!

IT CAN'T BE...

IT...

ARE YOU CONNECTED TO WHATEVER IS HAPPENING OUT IN SPACE?

WHO ARE YOU?

DAM-MIT!

SORRY FOR BEING SO QUICK ON THE DRAW. THAT'S ON US.

...

WE'RE JUST YOUR FRIENDLY NEIGHBORHOOD ALIENS, PASSING THROUGH.

WHAT ARE YOU TALKING ABOUT?

WE WON'T BOTHER YOU NONE, SO PLEASE LET US GO, OKAY?

SMART THINKING AS ALWAYS, BRO!

THAT'LL BE OUR CHANCE TO MAKE OFF WITH THE BLUE AURUM.

MORO'LL BE ITCHING TO TAKE THIS PLANET ONCE WE SEND WORD.

WE'RE REALLY JUST GONNA SLINK OFF?

174

FLIK

WE SURE AIN'T.

IT'S CLEAR YOU THREE AREN'T THE SOURCE OF THE GREATER DISTURBANCE.

FWOOM

!

SHLUFF

AND NEVER COME BACK.

GO ON.

MUCH APPRECIATED, GREEN FELLA.

DON'T LET THEM GET AWAY, PICCOLO!!

W-WAIT, NO.

HMM? SOMETHING'S FLYING AWAY.

THEY'RE ALLIED WITH THE GANG CAUSING TROUBLE OUT IN SPACE!

WHAT?

DENDE ?!

SOME-ONE ELSE?

VWOOOM

NO THANK YOU.

WE'D BETTER HURRY.

KAZOOSH

TCH!

BWAM

GAHHH !!

BOOM

ZOOM

KRASH

UGH ...

178

ZOOSH

IF THEY HAVE BEEN KILLED, THE PLANET THEY FOUND MUST BE HOST TO STRONG BEINGS INDEED.

HMM...

WHAT DO WE DO, LORD MORO?

INCOMING MESSAGE FROM THE MACARENI GANG. THEY SAID, "HELP US," THEN GOT CUT OFF.

WHAT NOW, SAGANBO?

I GUESS SO.

IT'S WORTH VERIFYING.

IF IT PROVES TO BE A QUALITY PLANET, I WILL DEVOUR IT MYSELF.

SEND A STRONGER SCOUTING PARTY.

AS THE FORCES OF DARKNESS ENCROACH UPON THE EARTH, GOKU AND MERUS BEGIN TRAINING...

182

SUCH IS ULTRA INSTINCT.

...IN THE FACE OF A JARRING SHOCK TO YOUR EMOTIONS.

IT WILL ACTIVATE WHEN YOU ACHIEVE SELF-CONTROL...

I'M SURE YOU HAD A REASON.

NO NEED TO BE SORRY.

YES...

YES.

YOU KNEW ABOUT IT ALL ALONG?

BEEP

SHWP

I APOLOGIZE FOR KEEPING THIS FROM YOU.

I ALREADY KNOW YOU'RE A GOOD GUY AND YOU WANNA BEAT MORO AS BAD AS ME, YEAH? THAT'S GOOD ENOUGH FOR ME.

TOTALLY FINE-- SAY NO MORE.

WE DON'T HAVE ALL THE TIME IN THE WORLD.

SO FORGET ALL THAT, AND LET'S GET BACK TO TRAINING.

FOLLOW ME, GOKU.

ANY DOUBTS I HAD ARE GONE NOW.

VERY WELL.

KREEK

WHAT THE ...?

OH YEAH?

SO NO HOLDING BACK IN HERE?

I WILL IMPART ALL I HAVE TO YOU.

THOUGH IT WON'T BE EASY. ARE YOU PREPARED?

FWP

FSSH

I WAS BORN READY!

FWP

TMP

OH? I CAN HARDLY IMAGINE.

AND THEN, ANOTHER SAIYAN SHOWED UP, BUT GET THIS-- HE WAS WAY STRONGER THAN US.

GALACTIC PATROL HQ: GOKU SUMMARIZED RECENT EVENTS ON EARTH FOR MERUS.

FREEZA CAME TO EARTH LOOKING FOR THE DRAGON BALLS, AND HE BROUGHT BROLY WITH HIM.

YEAH. HIS NAME IS BROLY.

SPECIAL COMIC

HE KEPT GETTING STRONGER AND STRONGER AS WE FOUGHT, UNTIL HE FINALLY TURNED INTO A SUPER SAIYAN.

ONCE HE TRANSFORMED, WE COULDN'T EVEN BEAT HIM IN OUR SUPER SAIYAN BLUE FORMS, SO ME AND VEGETA HAD TO PERFORM FUSION.

SOME-HOW, WE WON.

HOW DID HE END UP THERE?

VAMPA?! THIS FELLOW LIVES IN SUCH A HOSTILE ENVIRON-MENT?!

TO A PLANE-TOID CALLED VAMPA.

I DON'T THINK HE WAS ACTUALLY A BAD GUY... ANYWAY, HE WENT BACK HOME.

W-WAIT! WHERE'S HE NOW? WHAT IF DECIDES TO COME BACK FOR MORE...?

I FOR-GET.

DUNNO. DO YOU REMEM-BER, VEGETA?

NO... I FEEL AS THOUGH THIS MUST BE MY FATHER'S FAULT, SOME-HOW...

MAYBE HE JUST LIKES LIVING IN SUCH A NASTY PLACE. WHAT A WEIRDO.

THESE TWO COULDN'T HAVE KNOWN ABOUT THE GRAND TALE WEAVED BY THEIR PARENTS' GENERATION...

(ORIGINALLY APPEARED IN JUMP VICTORY CARNIVAL 2019 OFFICIAL GUIDEBOOK)

YOU'RE READING
THE WRONG WAY!

Dragon Ball Super reads from right to left, starting in the
upper-right corner. Japanese is read from right to left,
meaning that action, sound effects, and word-balloon
order are completely reversed from English order.